T0082750

Poetry Garden Bloom

Poetry Garden Bloom

A Collection of Poetry

Eileen Fierro

POETRY GARDEN BLOOM
A COLLECTION OF POETRY

Copyright © 2020 Eileen Fierro.

All rights reserved. No part of this book may be used or reproduced by any means, graphic, electronic, or mechanical, including photocopying, recording, taping or by any information storage retrieval system without the written permission of the author except in the case of brief quotations embodied in critical articles and reviews.

iUniverse books may be ordered through booksellers or by contacting:

iUniverse
1663 Liberty Drive
Bloomington, IN 47403
www.iuniverse.com
844-349-9409

Because of the dynamic nature of the Internet, any web addresses or links contained in this book may have changed since publication and may no longer be valid. The views expressed in this work are solely those of the author and do not necessarily reflect the views of the publisher, and the publisher hereby disclaims any responsibility for them.

Any people depicted in stock imagery provided by Getty Images are models, and such images are being used for illustrative purposes only.
Certain stock imagery © Getty Images.

ISBN: 978-1-6632-0615-2 (sc)
ISBN: 978-1-6632-0617-6 (hc)
ISBN: 978-1-6632-0616-9 (e)

Library of Congress Control Number: 2020914128

Print information available on the last page.

iUniverse rev. date: 08/12/2020

For Serafin,
for Remie
and for Keagan Fierro
… mi amores, mi vida.

A Dedication to Readers

This book started out as a way to organize a pile of loose paper, but it has become something much more. It has become my first steps on a journey to become an author. I have always loved to put words together in some creative or meaningful way. Choose to read this book in any way that you like, from cover to cover or by single pages when you are so inspired. It is an honor to share my thoughts scribed into poetry for you. My hope is that anyone who picks up this book is able to find a small piece of him or herself in some of the selections or maybe just an understanding for a different perspective of many lifetime experiences. Sit down, turn the cover and enjoy the words.

CONTENTS

LIFETIMES

DEATH

POETRY GARDEN

Edna for fire,
Sylvia and sorrow,
Anna, you're a survivor
and Emily, love letters:
Death shapes your verse
into craft like no man
with a hammer in his hand;
and as lexicon lay
abandoned to a page
covered in cardboard
sentenced to shelf life
by the turn of a page,
your resurrection occurs.
Transgressing generations
you are still heard
with all sultry sentiment
and the muted power
of your living dead words.

STORYTELLER

HOME WRECKER

I am not afraid.
I am a child of God.

Silence seeps from ruins,
but I hear planes
wrecking the horizon.
Footfalls came to our door.
One shot struck the dark;
I won't see Papa anymore.
Mama hid me for the bomb.
The slow black night turned to day.
Peek-a-boo from my heap.
Far away I see her face,
a gun deep in her back.
She walks away from me…
I won't see Mama anymore.
I climb a pile of rubble
to see what is still there.
If anyone is hiding,
they do not stir.
I yell out to empty space,
because I am not a soldier
but I might die like one.

I am a child of God
and I am not afraid.

URBAN CAMPER

His shadow looms large on the building wall
like a beast would stalk a concrete jungle.
Sun going down on another day,
dusk is a little spooked.
Dark and darker, fall and falling
No one knows where he has been.
No one knows where he is going.
The faces at night begin to change;
pimps, dealers and freaks take the streets.
The rest are left to fend for themselves.
Shuffling towards the outskirts of town,
he hunts and gathers food on the way.
He arrives at the roaring underpass;
a few of his belongings are already stashed.
He clears away a pile of jagged green glass
and lays down his wrinkled blue tarp at last.

THE CHIEF

Indian eyes
never tell what they hide.
Black as the midnight sky
with a warrior's pride
those eyes stay dry.
The old forgotten chief
stoops by the riverside.
The creak of his joints cannot lie,
the fatigue of so many years gone by.
Barely, just barely, he is still alive.
His head lifts to the sound of a cry.
Lone Eagle rides the mountainside.
A shadow now appears way up high;
an arrow is pointed, it's ready to fly.
The old man could only sigh
and embrace Earth where his bones must lie
now and forever, while his spirit flies
up to the Eagle's wings,
with all his wisdom
and he now dies.

SPEED

Runaway train,
taking me so fast,
so far from there.
Wish I was on the inside
'stead of hanging out here.
This runaway train,
so out of control.
Emotions riding high,
I just don't know.
I swear Runaway Train
no more trouble from me.
Bless you for taking me away
but I've got to live to be free.
Runaway train,
you've got to slow down..
can't hold on any longer
...still miles from town.

SUICIDE CAROUSEL

The most colorful array of circular lights
only adds to the dark of her pitch-black night.
Abandoned now, everyone has gone home
with the happy face clowns, and she is alone.

A stampede of animals, run around, run around.
Nausea turning... it's up, then it's down.
Make-up runs wrinkles across her baby face;
the operator's booth, hollow with empty space.

Cotton-candy music sounds sickeningly sweet,
the notes of the children's songs don't miss a beat.
Her blood-stained wrists slip down the center pole;
sacrifice the vessel, lose a vice for the soul.

The carnival and a carousel, it's meant for fun and play,
but if this is a game; and this is her life,
she doesn't care to stay.

IRISH FIGHTER

It's a tombstone in the hall; shock
forms small caverns of black
hollow holes on blank faces.
It's Mickey, again,
at the end of the twelfth,
when he shoulda' gone down in ten.

It is spar for spar
for the unlucky foe in the ring,
because he will be the one to pay
for Mickey's drunk mom, out cold on the stoop
and a father who turns bolts on the door.

Four corners of the ring have collapsed;
the rules of the game don't apply.
He is still swinging irons for fists
at an opponent, who has long gone home,
checked out now into deep space.

But Mickey is still up for the fight
turning the white noise back to black
and seeping red in a bloodbath
staining those tough streets again
at the corner of Brooklyn and Main,

The last warrior on the battlefield
counts it as a victory for the army
of one; it's lonely at the top
for prizefighter-fisted Mickey
standing now, like a lion over his prey.

MATADOR

Mine is only one of two daring faces inside of this ring;
the end of this match will be the end of another's suffering.
Armed with a mad-red muletta and a silver-tipped sword,
I demand command of leering fate.
I taunt, I tease, with no apparent unease,
I beg to bring this brute slowly to his knees.
I am quick; I am able; I am everything he is not

...but, there is a slow-mounting fury inside his protruding chest
into furious with every hot breath.
My eyes stay fixed like an invitation,
while his thick head bends brooding low.
One hoof rakes a line in loose dirt,
two horns point to steer the charge,
all four feet never reach the ground;
but, there is an approach of undeniable sound.
I know what it is that I now must do
to prove who is strongest of us two.
I raise this sword high up over my head;
there is just this one chance to see this bull dead.

IMMIGRANT VERSE

I.

A battered leather suitcase was left on the platform,
when the heavy train slowly pulled itself away.
The wail of a child's cry and the whistle outside
were lost to a distance that fell in between.

II.

In the guise of uncertainty, day has become night.
but you still follow each long mile ahead.
Your only provision for any source of light...
a dim-lit future for many promises left unsaid.

III.

Mexico is a country not so far from here,
but it may be for whom the question is asked.
Recipes and stitches can come across the border,
but, the dirt is fresh and will need to be tilled.

IV.

America was born in generations;
you turned your passport in at the door.
Your culture is all but confiscated.
Any word for 'home' won't make it your own.

V.
Daughter, granddaughter, you're speaking in tongues;
you are the foreigners to me.
I open my mouth and nothing comes out.
In this silence, I wonder how far it is I've come...

VI.
The suitcase remained at the abandoned station,
in a state of continuous decay over time.
The contents eventually spilled over the ground
to identify someone now only known as gone.

VII.
Delicate handkerchiefs sewn in crochet,
the iron press must have been for her best dress.
The cost of these items was more than she could afford
for a woman without country, land or home.

ABANDON AND FORGIVE

It cracked as she spoke in the dark of the room
waking the young man in the chair with a start.
"Will you forgive me for what I have done?"
The voice sounded almost foreign to him...
and he almost wished that it had been;
been words from the mouth of almost anyone
and not from the woman resting still next to him
because then it might have been easier to know
just what it was she was really asking for.

The overstuffed chair suddenly grew grand in size
or the man that he was, was once small again:
It was one day of the year when the guests had come,
all of the guests, except for one.
There had been games and colorful balloons in the air.
Half-eaten plates of vanilla frosting cake
still littered the plastic lining on the dining table.
The boy sat still on cushions in the sill
waiting for the sound of hurried clicks
to fall on red bricks up the path
to the open front door.

He remembered his friend Barry broke the chain on his new bike
and that had been so easy to forgive.
He remembered the favorite toy that his grandmother forgot to buy
and that too, he had been able to forgive.
He remembered his teacher put the wrong mark on his paper,
"everybody makes mistakes"...so he had had to forgive.
But for many long days, he sat there still..
listening for the clicks..

to fall on bricks..
up the path..
to the open door.

Morning sun broke through the small window pane
and fell in gold streams on the starch white sheets of the bed.
It almost made her ill-withered body look angelic...
but there was no halo and he was no fool.
Two decades and a few years separated him from the bed
on the day that could easily be her last
and he stood up without finding a single word to say
to this woman without any clicks to fall on red bricks..
leading up a path to an open front door.

SENTIMENTS

RIVER ROCK

A block of earth
undone, unmoving,
a chiseled face
drawn by sand and water;
the two forces combined
are stronger than itself.
It's a character sketch
made of dark markings,
birthmarks of origin.
For thousands of years,
lacerations reveal
testaments of time.
The stories unfold
from embedded fossils,
eternally entombed
in the solidity
of the steadfast
petrified river rock.

BLOOD OF THE AMARYLLIS

A Christmas gift
from bulb to bloom,
red veins course on canvas.
Like the knife
that pierced her heart,
what is want
to unwanted.
Crimson color
and splendor drops
the eye of the beholder.

HALLOWEEN NIGHT

It is the time of year when
shadows cast over summer sun.
Memories drawn in lined-up ghosts
in the haze of a haunting dream.
Nostalgia envelopes me like a hearth fire.
The smell of bones or burnt leaves
bring home to time in a capsule
and will keep yesterday for a moment today
on Halloween night quite unlike my rest.

MIRAGE

The presentation, the condition
of what we believe
worthy of admiration, or affection
lies wrapped in the human condition.
This apparition,
an apparent deception
of fault and fallacy
bestowed upon all generations
becomes the betrayal of an essence
to be human above all
which is the embodiment
of creation and what we are meant to be.

FISSURES IN THE GLASS

Life, by all appearances,
it is a perfect work of art
delicately crafted,
like it is a vase
almost too pretty for something more so inside.

The clarity, almost blinding
in its immaculate condition
allows for a vision
something like a dream
of hope, inspiration
of anything that it can be.

Wind and stone to sand
sun and ice to water
weathered and worn to wear
or something like a tragedy
are all too much for insecurity.

Fissures form caverns of small veins
on this flawless work of art.
They amplify themselves
like cancer cells
into a new design.

The vision becomes distorted
fractured and confused.
Now, this perfect work of art,
comes in a disguise
like it is now a ceramic mask
that cannot be touched
without first being destroyed.

THE UNKNOWING

I knew it was three in the afternoon,
but the damn rooster kept on crowing.
The tops of trees tickled and rippled
like a river moving over rocks in air.
A dog smiled and walked with his man
once again, on a twisting cement road.
Then, a slow, low down car crawled by
vibrating muffled sounds and rolling rims in reverse.
For the time of a moment within the hour,
a seeming unknowing took over me.
My fresh eyes drop with a spring green leaf
as it swirled down on to a dusty ground.

CARMELBYTHESEA

Step into a picture book,
southbound to a town where
the secondhand will forget to move.
Carmelbythesea....
floats inside a seasalt bubble,
and sheltered by a canopy
of green jade cypress trees.

Cacophony from the world outside
blends into pleasant harmony.
Slow shuffles saunter past
storefront taffy-candy windows
that curl down Ocean avenue
to a white soft granulated beach
dressed in its' best, blue
sun-sparkle Pacific Ocean water.

LOVE & WAR

THE CHASING GAME

Love chases..
like dogs with tails.

I'm looking at you,
you're looking at her
(with a glance back to me),
she looks at you,
when you look at me;
he looks at her
and one or two more
look fancy at me.

Love chases..
like dogs with tails

LOVE LIKE SICKNESS

"Doctor! You've come...
the infection has spread
throughout my body
but it has ...
such...such a...
sweet numbing sensation.
And to feel as if,
I am not in touch with the earth
but floating so far apart;
this puts me ill-at-ease.
Listen...closer to me...
palpitations of my heart.
Please, stop this spinning head!
Through these glazed eyes..
I see things I imagine are true,
Could this really be simply meant for me?
Alas! What is it you say?
A sickness known as the only as its kind.
That one for the want of a man
to be only ever called.. mine?

INFECTION

His invading presence
impressed itself upon my mind,
a residence of another kind,
and spread itself like a disease
that threatens to stay another day.
Infected by a profound desire;
a curious want remains.
Tantalizing tentacles of possibility
tickle me under thin skin.
It is kind of fun really
to be in the giddy
of a hopeless infatuation.

HOUSE OF CARDS

No architect would rest a roof
upon a house of cards
for shelter from those haunts,
that beckon you...
calling you and calling you,
wanting to break you down.

All that you have built him to be
will come crashing down.
And left bereft, you stand alone...
a refugee among the shards.
Nothing is left but a pile of cards,
and there is no space inside.

DIAMONDS CUT DEEP

Rock crystal clear
cut from downward
strikes in ground
up to meet
a heart for heart
on surface burning
touch sky high
and then brooding low.

Love left still,
undefined and broken
rules apply
still, heartbeat
in poignancy.
She left him
the message
for dead ears.

THE NIGHT AFORE WAR

This night lit by its own device,
a dramatic accumulation of sky,
speckles of metallic shards
look more and more just like stars.
An onslaught of inflated clouds
crowd the darkness that lay ahead.
From the distance falling behind,
illuminations show what's passed.
And at the end of all of this?
The tin soldiers will keep marching.

THE KING IS DEAD

These vast rolling pastures filled with riches and green
lay in the dead hands of our once great king.

The king lay still upon his regal bed
only one hour from which he was dead.

The widowed queen stoops in a heap of sorrow;
forty days to mourn will begin tomorrow.

All the king's men scatter now to and fro
in a state of confusion of which way to go.

"The will! The will! Will show us the way!
of who's to be crowned on this sad day!"

The fate of this blessed golden land
is now left to a singularly chosen man.

selected by our poor fallen king,
whose silence now is most unsettling.

THE KILLING OF KOSOVO

Macabre
massacre.
Target One,
no name
no face.
It's a place
to kill.
The killing
killers
kill
two survive;
guns
point
blank.
Killer instinct,
I feel nothing.

THE LAST SOLDIER'S RETURN

The 108ᵗʰ US Battalion was now soldiered by one.
The sticky mass of his golden hair stuck glued to the ground.
His good blue eye resigned itself to look forever towards a
dusty sky.
A hot crack in the earth singed his open skull wound,
he cursed the damn desert in one feeble motion to the side.
Now that eye rest upon a wrinkled pair of leather strapped feet.
He strained to listen to the messiah's voice as he began to speak:

"I am King Nebuchadnezzar II, I welcome your return to this ancient land.
When you are able, we will walk inside these four thick walls
to the hanging gardens of my enchantress, Amytis
to reinstate the life of your soul destroyed by this unholy war.
As the water of the great Euphrates River feeds the roots of great giant palms,
and weaves wet streamers in the hair of vines
and the softest shower of mist crystallizes in air,
go climb high to the top of the pillared terrace stairs
to repossess the vision of your own life and feats.
Generate purity for your spirit life through atonement;
then sweet maidens will guide you into a realm of time transcendent from
what you now know.
to enjoy the heavenly and holiest of this great pleasure,
relinquish your spirit's vessel, lying there weak and defeated, broken and
unmoved."

One breathless gasp sucked burnt air over his split lips.
He blinked hard and broke the seal of the encrusted eye;
two eyes now searched over a futile mile of barren brown land,
witness only to a haze of white sun and swirling sand.
Much nearer were two large footprints fossilized in dirt.
The soldier surrendered for this one reason he had come,
to find his final rest in the Hanging Gardens of Babylon.

OAKLAND SENTIMENTS

This mus' jus' be my day.
Two eyes blink above the barrel.
I am looking at a solid rim of steel.
I see a rising ring of smoke
and then I can smell it too,
just before this golden bullet
leaves it's chamber bed
to rest itself again
only inside my head.
Will I die as fast as I have lived?
"Mother, may I…?"
I can see everything now.
These city streets are as hard
as this grey cool pavement.
I think if I can jus' turn around,
I'll go to the other side of town.
God….
if I can live just one more day.

JAMES HOLMES AND TWELVE

Look! Look! Take a long look…
look at the bloody mess and what you have done.
It's a massacre, James; you've taken their lives.
The innocent lives of so many more than one.

Look closely at your reflection, James.
Try to understand what it is that you see.
It is not the devil looking back at you, James.
It's a mirror; it's you, and all you will ever be.

And you are not The Joker, James.
That was crude make-up applied to your face.
The mask is gone; there's no door to escape.
You're still in the theatre, alone in empty space.

You should listen to your lawyers, James.
Your only defense will call you crazy, totally insane.
And that is the greatness of this irony, James;
you're an inmate to the madness of your own sick brain.

Those beautiful faces that circle you, James
will remain forever in a fate you took upon yourself.
And for the rest of all your miserable long days,
the screaming devil in the mirror is multiplied by twelve.

LIFETIMES

MOTHER ALICE

Marry, maternity, mother and leave
Oceanic seascape
To tempestuous tides
Hurl, swirl, swipe and swallow
Empty the bottle...
Rewind the reel

Absolved of cruelty, crime and contempt,
Leopoldina has died.
Images sentenced to pictures
Children have eyes
Emotions purge and come clean

DOWN THE CANYON

These dirt-rigid walls won't give anything,
I'm diminished by narrowed rock and sand.
Stillness is mummified like an ancient ancestor
with a disturbing disregard for the decency of time.

The wide, empty riverbed died of dehydration
and now is an abscess infecting the land.
Aging shadows sweep down in painted arches
in procession with night's crusade over day.

I take a long look for any familiar signs of life,
and someone who came before me remains.
My fear is shaped like a trophy in the dark
that has won the surrender of another desert day.

ALL THE KINGS HORSES AND MEN

It's a nursery rhyme.
The child is wounded,
left to age in pieces,
stunted and broken,
in two separate parts
that remain integrated,
like the yolk to the egg.
It's all too much
for the kings horses and men
who need a new ending it seems.
Poor Humpty Dumpty
will have to find means
to put himself back together again.

GHOST OF A MAN

The cement headstone, Mariner, still rests in place
in the designated plot of space
where your seafaring bones must lie.

Within the tomb of caked-on dirt
these old bones lay still, neat and orderly,
to narrate the story of a day that came
when the ink was drawn for your shipping papers.

An agonizing separation, an ascension, of
your ethereal soul from your sickly body
commemorated your final living breath,
a sentence of which you now still serve.

In the decree of death,
you are left to wander, eternally
like a homeless vagrant, a vagabond
on seven masses of wretchedly-parched land.

For so many more centuries on end
᾿ every living day will give it's way
to the everlasting sun in an attempt to bring you down
to the dredges of a moisture-starved ground.

And for you, there will always exist
a mad and restless search for the sea
your tortured soul may become brittle
like mud turning into cracks on earth.

Hopefully, your soul will break itself to pieces
combust into mere molecules,
and you will become in union with air.
And as you pass by this hole in the dirt
there is a girl; it's your daughter, me
and I am standing there.

MOTHER BIRTH

As if I were human,
a thick skin wraps around my bones.
It is a product of your own creation,
but you are nowhere to be found.

I looked at you for the very first time
in a desperate search
for any beacon of recognition;
but you stare with two black holes for eyes.

The light of my life is lost to these pits of black;
darkness smothers me with two unearthly arms.
The center of my universe just banished me to deep space.
In a free fall, I am so violently pulled away
from the axis that spins the Earth around the Sun.

I have become an orphan in orbit.
There exists no connection of time to space.
Planets of outstanding color pass before and after me,
and I am a spectacle, an alien life form,
instead of the baby girl who I was meant to be.

TWO BLINKS OF AN I

The tree stands
stoic and proud,
so sure of itself.
Would that be me
if I were the tree?

Your arms enfold me
like 's' and 'ed'
on the ends of seduced.
Yet an ink stain will leave
permanence too.

CHILD ASLEEP

Rainbow colors of a day fall over hills to an end.
Stars connect in dots across a closing twilight sky;
and a crescent moon sings to you like any baby lullaby.
Your pudgy-pinch arms and legs lay quiet, still, at rest
and sleep carries you gently to a world of gumdrop dreams.
My mothering eyes look into your pure and innocent face
and I pull the soft blanket up closer to your chin.
Turning to go out the door, I'll leave a nightlight on.
The time has come to find my own bed
because everything is as it should and always be.

AMPM ADOLESCENCE

We're all just standin' around.
Thinking we are so cool,
but knowing we are really not.
Kinda' wishing we could be anybody,
except who we really are.
Maybe to be like Jules.
Who's talkin' to the older guys
like it doesn't even matter,
because they are so much cooler
than Richie and us over here.
His orange crusty fingers
keep pulling Cheetos from the bag.
But we know what it's like for Jules
when her dad is home
and her mother is not.
It's not a better place;
she just has a pretty face.
The question is always the same.
"Where do you wanna go?"
"I dun'no."
So we just pretend like
there is some better place
than just bummin' around.
'cause the only thing we really know
is that we won't be going very far
because everyone is here
and no one even has a car.

AUTOBIOGRAPHY

Angular lines in mirrors,
cascade in streaming color
falling down a black shaft
for an eye's view
of intricate prisms,
of all shapes and design.

Kaleidoscope,
a rotation of hands,
in opposition,
two spheres of
dimension and degree
cast back to a focused eye
as a paradigm for life
so perfectly proportioned
to both elements,
time and space.

DEATH

TIMING

Another time of day, the opposite of dawn,
a slow-moving peace and stilling tranquility
stroke perfect purple color stains to tie dye sky
painting a setting for the ascending orb.

CANCER FLY

A day cast round a brightly lit sun
amid the backdrop of blue sky
and earth's green hills of grass and grain
continue to rotate in spheres of slow unrelenting time.

But through the lens of nature's eye
a seemingly small and insignificant incident
has just occurred to produce the gravest
of unwanted change and consequence.

A small black fly with globes for eyes
lands on the petal of a vibrant flower.
Upon its departure it leaves,
an element of germ; a germ
of unsuspected force and power
that festers and infects itself into a bigger life.

The petal remains innocuous, beautiful.
Unknowing, it is benign
to the dire effect
of this sole pariah's
growth and perseverance
toward destruction.

The germ slowly seeps and withdraws
any display of color and light
bestowed upon the petal
and moves quickly to infect its host,
the larger body, the flower.

Now a hostage,
the flower remains defenseless
against the determination
of this assassin
so sinister, so intent
upon taking a life for its own.

The evil in this greed leaves
no remains of life left for the flower.
All its petals and its stem
collapse into a brown decaying mass,
now void of any color
and hollowed into simply
matter and nothing more.

SUPERNATURAL:
ODE TO DYSTROPHY

Body, the forever and over again, fallible human body,
born a forsaken and doomed earthly creation.
You are alive, but what has become of you?
Merely, a spirit that thrives, in theory and in thought,
but the carelessness of your own maker
leaves you in a state of dilapidation and decay.
Biologic warfare waged inside your vessel,
that will leave only a bare trace of bones
to lie down on Earth to decay again once more
in the rampant destruction of nature, age and time.

but it is your soul, survivor,
left to defy the finitude of organs, blood, skin and bones,
and you will rise up again...
transformed by the very earth that destroyed you.
Layers of metal: zinc, copper, iron and ore
in fusion with dirt, water and fire,
will surround your bones in a cast like a reptilian shell.
You become a supernatural!
impenetrable to the imperfection that once brought you down.
Your return will complete your fate and destiny,
in a state so much greater and more powerful
than the small and weak human bodily form
that failed so miserably in your short human life.

THE LAST GUEST

A few guests still remained when
Dawn abruptly crashed Night's party.
Life began to sing The Mourning Song;
Innocence had since come and gone
long before Vitality left feeling sick.
With a slight nod to the solemn twins, Fatigue and Apathy,
elderly Energy made his way slowly to the door.
All the while, Hope continued to argue with Despair
while Fear danced around them, twirling dizzily on tiptoes.
And they could all still see that the last dark-cloaked guest
was still in the corner standing there.

DOWN THE MOON

My hurt eyes can only watch as the bold moon rises tonight
in a silent and disturbing perfect rhythm with time.
Its full-bodied confidence is humbling...but frustrating...
How can I question this? the order of nature, of all things that
be and, who are we? The human race...
more or less than seven billion ants crawling on dirt.
Can the simplicity of man ever come to understand
what it is that truly moves this moon in a circle tonight?

The crickets are in chorus and are singing a really sad song;
I still stare at this moon as if to challenge it to come down.
But defeated now, I wonder if I know anything at all.
Language falls short of words against a torrent of despair.
Pennies for tears spill over into this pool of futility.
I bring nothing to a fight against a power such as this...
for anyone to try to call it by a name is just a fool to me.
But that is all that I may be, if I am the one
to seek comfort from a cold, dark moon
which won't stop staring, glaring,
laughing and gazing, its pitying face
down, on me.

SHE REMAINS

A small smile remained
upon her hallowed face
several moments after
her last remaining breath
escaped the cracked lips
of her once vital and vibrant body.

We are ones left to remain
standing dumb around a lifeless bed;
remainders are reminders that she left behind,
to tell us a story for our own lives.

SUMMER OF SYLVIA

She said: "Take the bouquet away."
Why? "Flowers just die."
As if to say,
contained in the life of that bouquet
was a tragedy darker
than all of its colorful beauty.

THE LOST GOODBYE:
For Theron

I must have said it 10,000 times before
never thinking that one may be our last
but now that you have gone
remember every goodbye I said in the past.

Memories will hardly suffice
for what should be more living days;
the goodbye that I might have said, had I known,
was another thing stolen that terrible day.

So suddenly, time is my worst enemy,
though it may not exist for you anymore,
but all those words I would have said,
are lost like ghosts floating out an open door.

Printed in the United States
By Bookmasters